Walking With God
91 Days on Your Christian Journey

By Jameson Alston

Copyright© 2020 by Jameson Alston

Written by Jameson Alston

Cover design by Moore Graphics & Design

Interior format by Jameson Alston

All rights reserved. No part of this book may be reproduced in any form by any electronic or mechanical means including photocopying, recording, or information storage and retrieval without written permission from the author.

Printed in the United States of America

If not specified, scripture quotations are taken from the King James Version of the Bible.

Acknowledgments

To my Lord, and my best friend. You've brought me a long way from where I was, and you're still leading me. Thank you, Lord.

To my family, I love you, and ain't a thing you can do about it!

PSALMS 91

He who dwells in the shelter of the Most High will abide in the shadow of the Almighty.

I will say to the Lord "My refuge and fortress, my God, in whom I trust."

For He will deliver you from the snare of the fowler and from the deadly pestilence.

He will cover you with His pinions, and under His wings you will find refuge; his faithfulness is a shield and buckler

You will not fear the terror of the night, nor the arrow that flies by day, nor the pestilence that stalks in darkness, nor the destruction that wastes at noonday.

A thousand may fall at your side, and ten thousand at your right hand but it will not come near you.

You will only look with your eyes and see the recompense of the wicked. Because you have made the Lord your dwelling place---- The Most High, who is my refuge---

No evil shall be allowed to befall you, nor plague near your tent.

For He will command His angels concerning you to guard you in all your ways.

On their hands they will bear you up, lest you strike your foot against a stone.

You will tread on the lion and the adder; the young lion and the serpent you will trample underfoot.

"Because he holds fast to me in love, I will deliver him; I will protect him because he knows my name.

When he calls to me, I will answer him; I will be with him in trouble; I will rescue him and honor him.

With long life will I satisfy him and show him my salvation."

Dear Reader

Thank you for investing in your spiritual walk by getting this material. I pray it blesses you immensely. Before you begin this journey into the next season of your life, please keep a few things in mind.

This devotional should be a supplement to your daily bible readings, personal study of scripture, and prayer.

To maximize your experience with reading this material, please utilize the reflections pages to take notes or write out the thoughts that come to your mind as you go through each daily message.

Again, thank you, and I pray you experience a transformative journey in this next season of your life.

Day 1

Your Father is Calling

John 6:44

Dear Christian, God is calling you for great and mighty things. God has a plan for your life and wants to lead you on a journey to advance His Kingdom. In this process, we must get to know Him as our Heavenly Father. God wants a personal relationship with you. He wants you to know His will for your life and to trust Him with your purpose. God will guide you through life, and help you with decisions that must be made. He is your friend and your counselor at all times and will support you even when you have nothing left to stand on. God will speak to you. God will put people in your path to help you along the way. To hear Him more clearly, you have to get rid of distractions and set aside time just for yourself and God. The Father has wisdom, knowledge, and abundant grace at His throne. We as believers must get to know Him so we can receive everything he has for us. The Father is calling you dear Christian, to bring you into your calling. Follow the leading of His Holy Spirit and you will enter into your divine destiny.

Walk with God, Follow His Leadership, and He will show you marvelous things.

Reflections

Day 2

God Made You On Purpose

Ephesians 2:8-10

We often ask the question to ourselves many times, "what am I here for?" or "what is my purpose in life?" God has purposed us to be in this world because we are needed to manifest the work He put in us to do. By the very evidence of your birth, you are needed because you were born with a purpose from God that the world needs. The Greek work for workmanship in this verse is the word "poiema" which is where we get the word poem from. You, dear Christian, are God's poem. You came from His heart and his hands. He created you for good works that he prepared for you before the world had a beginning. So today, live your life like you were made to live it; on purpose. What better purpose than God's plan for you?

Your breath is evidence you've got Purpose For Today!

Reflections

Day 3

Get to Know God

Ephesians 2:4-6

When you talk about God, people oftentimes think of this great, large ghost in the sky, who doesn't really care about you but requires your obedience and is quick to wrath. The Bible makes it clear that God is not like that. Rather, He (The Creator of the universe) wants to hear from you. He wants to spend quality time with you. God wants you to include Him into every area of your life. God already knows everything about you. He knows your family, He knows what you really like, and what you really don't care for, He knows what you did last summer. He loves you. Yes, God loves you! Even when you don't brush your teeth because you're running late for work, God still wants to be up close and personal with you! You don't have to work for God's love, His favor, or His acceptance. He loves you because you are His. He wanted you to be born, and He placed you in this day that He made you to experience His goodness. All he wants is for you to trust Him. He believes that there is a better, a greater, and an ever increasing life for you, why not agree with Him and allow Him to lead you into it?

Get Close to God, and He will get Close to you.

Reflections

Day 4

AMAZING Love

Mark 12:30-31

Dear Christian, as you embark on this journey, there are many things that are going to come your way. However, to respond to it all properly, there's only one thing you must do. That my friend, is LOVE. Yes, I said it; love is the master key to it all. Love God with all of your heart, soul, mind, and strength; and love your neighbor as yourself. There is no greater commandment that God has given us than to **love**. This kind of love that Jesus talks about is not merely an affection or a fondness of something, but to have an unconditional sincere love towards God and your neighbor. Even when it's uncomfortable, God calls us to love the people around us just like He does. The Greek word for love here is "agape". Which is translated as "charity" in various translations because true love requires the action of giving. Think about this, with all the offenses we have made to God, He STILL chooses to love us, and has GIVEN us His Son Jesus Christ, who GAVE Himself for us to be with our Heavenly Father. Love is so powerful because it caused God to give us Himself, FULLY and without restraint even though we are undeserving. God's love for us is so amazing, He saw all of our flaws and still chose to send Jesus to die for us and then bless us with His Grace and Mercy.

God's Love for You is AMAZING!

Reflections

Day 5

The God of All Comfort

2nd Thessalonians 2:16-17

There is no greater comfort than the one we have as Christians: knowing that Our God REIGNS. He cares for us. He is the God of comfort meaning that He will console you, protect you, and guide you throughout your life. Through God's grace we have access to hope that the world does not have. We have peace with God [Romans 5:1] through Jesus Christ. In other words, because of Jesus, we are in good standing with God the Father. Because of Jesus, we are privileged to experience Gods love and His Holy presence at all times. Have you ever thought about how much God loves you? Have you ever considered to comprehend the peace and comfort you feel being in God's Holy Presence? Dear Christian, be comforted in knowing that God is with you, comforting you, and helping you reveal His goodness to the world in everything you do.

Be comforted by God's Grace as you Walk with Him Today.

Reflections

Day 6

Complete in Christ

Colossians 2:10

God made us to be beautiful. When sin came into the world, we became broken. Now we struggle internally with insecurities, fear, doubt, discontentment, etc. We constantly try to make ourselves complete through relationships, material possessions, and obsession for fame. We chase fulfillment in creation, when we neglect that fulfillment is only found in the creator. God Himself came to earth as the man Jesus Christ to make you complete in Him. You don't have to chase relationships to be made whole or be complete. You are only made complete through relationship with God, which only comes through Jesus Christ [John 14:6]. You don't need another car or another house, or be in a higher tax bracket to be fulfilled in life. Get to know God personally and experience fulfillment every day.

Experience God today!

Reflections

Day 7

God Is With You

Philippians 2:13

On this journey there is one BIG thing you have to keep in mind. God will never leave you by yourself!!! Everything God has for you to accomplish, He is working in and with you to make sure that it happens. He works in you the desire to see it accomplished, and labors with you to bring it to pass. David spoke of God's faithfulness saying that if he "made his bed in Hell, God would be with him" [Ps. 139:8]. No matter what the struggle or situation is, God is with you. Both bright and gloomy days are not absent of God's presence. Always remember that God is faithful. Stay close to Him and trust Him with everything. When you desire what God desires for your life, God is working with you to bring it to pass.

God began a good work in you, and He is faithful to finish it!

Reflections

Day 8

God's Got A Plan

Joshua 1:8

The Bible is an instruction manual for skillful living. The Word of God is living and active [Heb 4:12]. There are 783,137 words in the Bible written to man by a God who wants His people to be secure, safe, and sustained. There are so many principles found in God's Word that if applied to one's life will be found highly beneficial. In God's Word, we find truth that is applicable to every area of our lives. From family, friends, feelings, and finances, there are principles in God's Word that are designed to steer us in the right direction and have a successful life. However, we have to get in the Word and apply it before we can reap the harvest of the Word. [Matt 6:33] Remember this acronym: BIBLE= Basic Instructions Before Leaving Earth.

You can't go wrong going with God's Plan.

Reflections

Day 9
Planted to Prosper

Psalms 1:1-3

The best place to plant a tree is by water. Water is what nourishes the roots for the tree to grow and become settled in the ground. A tree that's settled on good ground doesn't have to worry about becoming uprooted by storms or being contaminated by weeds. A tree that's planted near water is in perfect conditions. It doesn't have to worry about having enough nourishment to produce nor about the seed being choked. All the tree does is what it is created to do namely, produce fruit. Staying rooted in God's Word will have you planted like the tree in the set place, at the set time, doing what you were made to do, yielding fruit for all to taste the goodness of the Lord.

Being planted in God's presence produces a fruitful life

Reflections

Day 10

Transformation

Romans 12:2

As you embark on your spiritual journey, one thing you can't forget is that you've been "made new in Christ." This means that certain things the world does, you don't do. You are not like the world. You can't forget who you are. You're a new creation in Christ Jesus. There are some things that you can't hold on to any longer because they're holding you back from living in your purpose. Now that you are changed, your mindset has to change. The word transformed in Romans 12:2 holds the image of a caterpillar that goes through the cocoon phase, and is now transformed into a butterfly. You are like the butterfly, made new in Christ. No longer a caterpillar. A butterfly doesn't have the same mindset as a caterpillar. Be transformed by the renewing of your mind means you as the butterfly cannot keep living caterpillar-ish. God wants us to be totally transformed by His Word.

Confess this daily: I am no longer the same In Jesus name, Amen.

Reflections

Day 11
REST

Exodus 33:14

Everything that functions properly needs rest. Birds need rest. Cars need rest. Bears rest for up to 7 ½ months. Even TVs have sleep mode! Video games will run hot if overworked and begin to malfunction. God himself rested on the seventh day! We are no exception to needing rest. Our bodies need rest to function properly and be productive. Our bodies are temples for God's Spirit to DWELL, which literally is a place to REST[1st Corth 3:16][1st Corth 6:19]. Part of honoring God with our bodies is getting adequate rest. Slow down!!! You're running yourself ragged worrying about more things that matter less. Stop, reset, and stay centered on Christ. God will give you rest and peace on your Christian Journey.

Get some Rest!

Reflections

Day 12

You Play to Win the Game

1st Corinthians 9:24

As an athlete trains, strives, and seeks to win, we as Christians are to be determined, diligent, and disciplined in our lifestyle. Athletes represent the teams they play for and their identity is associated with the team. Today, consider who you represent with your actions. Can people recognize who you play for by the life you live? Do people associate your lifestyle with Christ? Athletes are always practicing, studying their playbook, and training to stay fit for the sport. They desire to win championships so they discipline themselves to obtain them. As Christians, we should have a desire to dominate in life. We should also discipline ourselves accordingly to receive what we want out of life. We have to study our playbook [The Bible], practice what we preach, and develop habits that honor God daily. A walk with God, regardless what you walk away from is always victorious. Today, dear Christian, play your position, and give God your best.

You have the victory in Christ [1st Corinthians 15:57]

Reflections

Day 13

Lights Please

Matt. 5:16

When I was a little kid, I never liked to go to sleep when it was completely dark. I always had to have a small light near my bed (don't judge me). I had a bad case of "Nyctophobia". Similarly, all of us have a fear of being "in the dark" about something. We have a fear of being stuck in this world with no hope or support. We fear failure or being trapped by the dangers that are present in this world around us. The good news is that God has given us light in Christ Jesus. Because of Jesus, we are no longer in the dark about what God is like. Because of Jesus, we don't have to walk in the darkness of sin. Because of Jesus, we no longer have to give into fear, rather we can overcome our fears with faith. Because of Jesus, we can show others the light in our lives which is Christ. That light within us shines brightest when we are content with our new found identity in Christ, and when we are willing to express ourselves in Him through our lifestyle. Letting your light shine, is allowing Christ's character to manifest through you.

This world on its brightest day is full of darkness. Jesus said, You are the light. Shine bright so others can see today.

Reflections

Day 14

Trust: A Solid Foundation

Psalm 125:1-2

The Hebrew word for trust in this scripture is "batach", and it literally means to have confidence, boldness, and assurance. God wants us to be assured of His faithfulness, bold in His righteousness, and confident in His strength. God wants you to trust Him with every area of your life. When things don't go our way we need an assurance of God's faithfulness to come through for us. Trusting God comes from knowing God, and knowing God comes from spending time with God. The more we trust God, the further we will go in our walk with God. Developing in faith and trust in God builds us up to be used by God. God will use you in your home, on your job, and in many different places to share His message. Trust in God is a foundation for every believer to live in faith for their purpose every day.

Trust in the Lord. He will take care of you.

Reflections

Day 15

An Eternal Guarantee

John 5:24

Dear Christian, every day, we are faced with several uncertainties. We wake up and the first things that typically comes to our minds are questions like, "What time is it?" or "where are my keys?" We have questions about events within the day, what we plan to do, or where we plan to go. Whether we're going to work or school, we are anxious about the next step. We're inquisitive about what lies ahead of us. For us students, we're constantly wondering what's going to be on our next test. For parents, you're wondering when your kids are going to get out the house. Teachers have questions about their students, and leaders have questions concerning their followers. Regardless of where we are in life, whatever our assignment is, we don't have to question or be worried about God going back on His Word. Jesus says "verily, verily" expressing assurance, that whoever hears Him and believes in God the Father will have everlasting life. We will not be condemned but passed from death to life. Dear Christian, when God promises us anything, we don't have to worry, it's a guarantee!

You have an eternal guarantee of God's love!

Reflections

Day 16

Diet for the spirit

1st Peter 2:2

When you think about babies, what comes to mind? They cry, they pout, and they make messes in their diapers. What else? They're always hungry for milk. Babies need milk to grow healthy and strong. When a baby is first born, they're alive, brand new in the world, but have no clue how to live in the world. In the same way, when you first received the gift of salvation, you're considered a babe spiritually. You need spiritual nourishment [The Word of God] so you can grow and mature. Milk is good for a baby to grow healthy and strong. Babies get multiple bottles throughout the day. Don't believe me? Ask someone with kids. In the same way a baby needs to frequently get nourishment from milk for their natural growth, we need to frequently get in God's Word so we can grow and mature spiritually. Throughout the day when you have down time (a lunch break, a trip to the car, or even at dinner), take every opportunity to get in God's Word on a daily basis!

We need God's Word for spiritual health and strength.

Reflections

Day 17

Rejoice in His Love

Jeremiah 15:16

When I was a kid, I loved doing stuff for my family. Performing in front of my family brought me so much joy. I loved it! From singing, dancing, and playing sports, I loved to bring my family joy and excitement. We're constantly reminded in the Bible to rejoice in the Lord. Here's why: Christianity is a relationship. Our Heavenly Father wants us to have confidence and excitement in Him [Who He is and what He can do]. He wants us to ENJOY His presence, and not feel forced to be with Him. He wants us to be EXCITED about our experiences and encounters with Him. Your heavenly Father wants us to rejoice in the things He has given us. Parents want their children to love them and enjoy their times together as well as be filled with joy. Dear Christian, God has called you by name for a perfect purpose and wants you to rejoice and be glad in the things He has done for you.

Rejoice and be glad in knowing who's walking with you.

Reflections

Day 18

Body Watch

1st Corinth 6:20

The human body is very unique. There are so many unique features your body has. Did you know the very structure of your brain changes when you learn something new? Did you know that your body can heal itself and produce its own antibodies to fight off foreign bacteria? Did you know the cells in your body are constantly being both degenerated and regenerated? About every three months, molecularly, your body is totally renewed. Your body is so unique! All of the joints, ligaments, tendons, and muscles function closely together for your purpose. This is why you can't do any and everything with any and every person. Your body is specially designed and it must be properly taken care of. Eating healthily, getting regular exercise, and rest are all key parts to taking care of your body. Your body is the Lord's Temple. You want to honor God in how you carry yourself daily. Don't abuse your body. You were bought with the price of the Blood of Jesus. Honor God with what you put in your body [food and substance], what you put on your body [clothes and accessories], and what you do with your body [activities and habits].

> Your body belongs to God.
> Honor Him with what He
> made.

Reflections

Day 19

One on One Time

Matt. 14:23

One of the most important components in the life of a Christian is prayer. Prayer is one of the central activities we see in the life of Jesus. As much as we see miracles, healings, teachings, and preaching, we see Jesus spending considerable amounts of time in prayer. Not only does He spend much time in prayer, looking more closely, we see Him getting **alone** to pray. Every relationship thrives through communication. Our relationship with God is no different. Prayer is communication with God, and when you commune with God one on one, you get exactly what you need from Heaven to complete your assignment. We can learn from Jesus how important it is to have one on one time with God. I encourage you, dear Christian, to open up to God, spend quality time with Him, and allow Him to show you things you have never imagined.

There's nothing like one on one time with the Creator.

Reflections

Day 20

Transformed Affections

Psalm 84:2

When I was in high school, one thing I was really passionate about was music. I loved playing and performing music. I loved learning about music, listening to music, listening to people talk about music. I really loved music. In middle school, while getting dressed, I would play my favorite songs all the way until I made it to school that morning. That passion for music motivated me to do a lot of things. Once I became a Christian, my focus became pleasing God through my music. The psalmist writes, His innermost desire is to be in the presence of God. That innermost desire should be ours as well. We all have things that we're passionate about, but nothing should matter more to us than being with God. God is so awesome and loving. We should desire to love him because of His love, grace, and mercy toward us.

Being in God's presence brings everything we need.

Reflections

<u>Day 21</u>

All Things Are Possible With God

Luke 1:37

Life has a way of presenting problems at every stage. Sometimes, we look at our problems and we immediately lose confidence or hope that the problem or obstacle can be overcome. God has reminded us hundreds of times in His Word of His faithfulness to us through His Grace. Our Father cares for us and will supply all of our needs according to His riches in glory by Christ Jesus [Phil 4:19]. God loves you more than you imagine. He will fight for you, and He will never leave you. He has made you more than a conqueror in Christ. We really can't count the number of times God has come through for us. I challenge you today to challenge your challenges with the truth of who your God is! He's the same God who created the universe out of nothing and will be the same at His Second Coming. God specializes in miracles, and with His Help, NOTHING is impossible!

> You can overcome ANYTHING
> when you're walking with God.

Reflections

Day 22

The Secret Place

Matthew 6:6

Our secret place is a private place we go for comfort, and peace. We tend to do in our secret place what we really want to do. It's where our real character is on full display. Jesus is often noted in scripture slipping away to pray alone in His secret place. We can see from scripture that communication with the Father is something that was really important to Jesus. If Jesus felt that talking with the Father was important to Him, it definitely should be important to us. The Bible says that when we pray to the Father in our secret place, then He will reward us openly. What we do in our secret place has our heart, and God wants to be the treasure in our heart. What we do in our secret place has top priority to us, and what we do in it determines what type of person we are when we come out of it. My brothers and sisters, God wants our hearts. The way we truly experience change is by giving Him our hearts in our secret place. The things we are seeking God for, the things we're asking God for, and the person God wants us to become is found in our secret place. When we give ourselves over to God in our secret place, our desires change, and we become more like Jesus. The secret place is the place of restoration, renewal, revelation, and transformation.

> Make Jesus your treasure, and give Him your Heart in the secret place.

Reflections

Day 23

God is my Source of Life
Acts 17:28

If I was to give you a cell phone, free of charge, fully equipped with apps, camera, facetime, unlimited minutes, and data that would be great right? You get the phone and begin to use it. Eventually the phone dies. Why did the phone die? It lost connection to its source of life. What is the first thing you do? You look for the charger to the phone. Why? Because the ONLY way a phone can receive life is if it's connected to its charger and plugged into the right source. God created you in His likeness and His Image. Because He created you, He is your source of life, and you cannot live the way you were originally intended to live being separated from Him. The only way we can get connected to God is through a loving relationship with Jesus Christ. Jesus is like the charger. No one goes before the Father without going through Christ (John 14:6). You can't charge your phone without a charger. The charger connects the phone to its life source. Jesus has come to connect us to the Father and His will for our lives. Invest some devoted time today in prayer, and in God's Word.

Plug in to your source and walk into your purpose Today!

Reflections

Day 24

God is my source of Identity

Psalms 139:14

Just a small thought: A mirror reflects the image.

Dear Christian, God has created, chosen, and called you to reflect His image. You were created to reflect God. You were chosen to *re-present* God. You were called to reveal God's grace to the world. "In His likeness and in His image" means you were made to act like Him and look like Him. "Wonderfully made" means, God made you full of wonder. You are the wonderful creation of God! "Fearfully made" means God was meticulous in your design. He was careful with how He made you. He specifically placed you in your family, ethnicity, and social demographic. You are so magnificently designed by God, no one on this planet has the same fingerprints as you, and no person in human history has had your fingerprints. This is God's testimony to you that what He has made for your hands to touch, no one else can take.

Show the world what God is like with your life.

Reflections

Day 25

God is my Source of Purpose

John 15:16,

God has called you to represent Him with your life. God wants you to give a LOT to Him. We give a LOT to our careers, relationships, school, and even church. Do we really give a LOT to God? A LOT stands for our Love, Obedience, and Trust. This is the purpose for your life. You were created to bring pleasure to God. To love, obey, and trust Him with your life. Regardless of vocation, we were all created to bring pleasure to God and give our LOT to Him. God created you, He knows what you were made to do and knows the path your life should take. Give God your LOT today. Start by thanking Him and acknowledging who He is. Let God take priority in your day. Center your day around your time with God and let Him lead you in the path towards His Promise for you.

> Get plugged into God, Get plugged into your purpose.

Reflections

Day 26

God is my source of strength

Ephesians 6:10

Have you ever seen those workout commercials showing before and after pictures? How do those people go from out of shape to in shape? How do these guys go from the diary of a wimpy kid to bodybuilder status? They commit themselves to the process that leads to the desired goal. It takes consistent commitment and active progression to develop natural strength gains in a workout. Likewise, it takes commitment of faith to be strong in the Lord. The difference between natural strength and spiritual strength is that natural strength cannot carry you over your obstacles when you're weak. Natural weakness is the absence of strength. Spiritual strength is not natural. This means even when you're weak, you are still strong. True strength is not how many times you can lift a weight, but it is the ability to live by faith and have joy, regardless of the tribulations that come to test you. We do not become strong by own efforts alone. We find true strength when we rely on the power of His grace that He has given us through His Son, Jesus Christ. We can do nothing apart from Jesus, but with Jesus we can do all things (Philippians 4:13, John 15:5). We need the grace of Jesus every day of our lives, and if we take our lives one moment at a time trusting in the power of Jesus' Grace that He's given us, we can accomplish anything God calls us to.

Jesus is the source of our strength

Reflections

Day 27

God is my source of power

Luke 10:19, Acts 1:8,

When a stick of dynamite is lit, it has so much power that it causes massive explosions and can literally change the landscape of the area surrounding it. Dear Christian, I have good news for you today. The Greek word for power in this scripture is the word *dynamis*, and it illustrates the power of a stick of dynamite when lit. Jesus has given you power for living. The power Jesus has given you is more powerful than all of the power of the enemy, and nothing that the enemy does can stop you in your pursuit of purpose. The power Jesus has given to you is meant to make you like that stick of dynamite, creating change in your area and shaking the world around you with the Gospel of Jesus Christ. It's power for you to live with every day. When challenging strongholds and walls of adversity attempt to capture you, the power of Jesus within you will enable you to tear down those strongholds, break through those walls of adversity, and live in freedom and victory.

> When you're plugged into God, you've got Power for Living!

Reflections

Day 28

Faith for Everything!

Mark 11:24

Believe, Believe, Believe!!! All you have to do is believe! There is nothing that can stop you from your destiny if you only believe! Faith is the assurance of things hoped for. Know that God has His hands on your life and take confidence and assurance that He will bring your hearts desires to pass. Don't be afraid to dream. Don't be afraid to fail. Don't let your fears overtake you, rather, overcome your fears with faith. Believe God for everything in your life. Whatever you desire, pray and believe you will receive and you shall have. Take the steps of faith through the doors set before you. Faith is something for everyday for everything! Sometimes it seems scary to step out on faith and trust God, but the more you spend time with God, the more your faith will grow. Use your faith and experience God in your life!

A Walk with God is a Walk of Faith!

Reflections

Day 29

The Gift that Keeps On Giving

2 Corinthians 9:15

You are blessed. You are abundantly blessed. You are exceedingly blessed. God has favored you to see this day He made full of opportunity and potential. God has made this day in completion and counted you NEEDFUL to be in it. EVERYTHING YOU NEED is in this day also. The word says that you won't find the righteous forsaken or begging because they lack (Psalms 37:25). Ladies and gentlemen, that's you because God shall supply ALL your needs according to His riches in glory by Christ Jesus [Philippians 4:19]. That means God will provide for you! You are blessed and you should thank God for the things you do have instead of complaining about the things you don't have! Before you complain, be thankful you have a breath to complain with. God did not just plan for you to be born and stop right there. He's working in your life right now. Christ has redeemed us from the curse of poverty, sickness, and spiritual death. God has given you a gift in Christ that will continue to give you more and more each day.

    You are abundantly blessed and highly favored

Reflections

Day 30

Faith Your Fears

Isaiah 43:1

When my sister was a little girl, she was afraid of the dark. If she ever had to go down the hall or go into a dark room, she would ask me to go with her or turn the light on for her. I started telling her that if I can't be there with her, Jesus would be there for her always. One day, I was outside and my sister wanted to go down the hallway, but it was dark. Usually, she would come outside and ask for me to go back inside with her. This day however, she went down the hall by herself and got her toys out of her closet. After she got her toys, she came running outside, screaming, "Brother, brother! Guess what? I went down the hall to get my toys. It was dark. I asked Jesus to go down the hall with me and protect me. He did, big brother! Look, I got my toys!" Just like my little sister, we too become afraid. We must remember, God did not give us fear. When we do become afraid, we have to put our faith and confidence in Jesus. Fear comes from the enemy to scare us from walking down the path God has for us. When we become fearful, we have to remember and acknowledge that God is with us, and there's nothing that can prevail against us. Whatever you're afraid of that's holding you back from experiencing the fullness of God for your life, know that Jesus is with you, and when He's with you, you have nothing to be afraid of.

It takes faith to face your fears.

Reflections

Day 31

Overcoming Temptations

1st Corinthians 10:13

Dear Christian,

In your walk with God you WILL face temptation. No question about it. The Bible lets us know we will face temptations. But these temptations are not impossible to overcome. God's word gives us assurance that we can do all things through Christ (Philippians 4:13). That includes enduring and overcoming temptations. Some people think that when you become a Christian, there will be no more temptations. Quite the contrary, when you become a Christian, it means that God is there to help us when we get tempted. Fortunately, God will not put more on us than we can handle. We have to remember God is faithful. With God, we no longer have to give into temptation, we now can overcome the temptation every time it's presented. Temptation is just an evil presentation to the mind. It's just as much an opportunity to do the right thing as it is to do the wrong thing. When we find ourselves tempted to sin or settle away from God, we also have an opportunity to obey and grow in God when we make the right decision. There is no temptation we face that is too great for God to deal with in our lives.

God is with us overcome our temptations.

Reflections

Day 32

You Are In The Family

John 1:12
Dear Christian,

How does it feel to know that you are in the family of God? Now that you have been born again, you are God's Child. It doesn't matter whether your natural parents were good parents or not, in your life or not. God has adopted into His family and you belong to Him now. Your heavenly Father is concerned about where you're headed in life. God wants His best for you as an earthly father would their children. Different from your earthly father, your heavenly father doesn't miss out on key points in your life. He always can give you the right advice, and when you call Him, He will never tell you He's too busy. He's given you a family of brothers and sisters to help you along your spiritual journey and hold you accountable. When people have children through conception, they don't choose their children; however, when a child is adopted, the parents actually CHOOSE their child. The Bible says that "God CHOSE YOU" (Ephesians 1:4) to be HIS CHILD. You are chosen by God to be HIS CHILD and represent Him on earth. Dear Christian, God is concerned about you. You have a good, good father in God.

Walk with your Heavenly Father!

Reflections

Day 33

Walking On Water

Matt 14:27

Dear Christian,

Walking with God will require you to go places that will seem uncomfortable at times. Like Peter, Jesus is bidding us to walk with Him. Many of us are like Peter in that, although we hear God's request, we look at the troubled waters and are afraid to walk with Him. Jesus gives us assurance today that regardless of the circumstance, regardless of what we are walking through, God wants us to know that we can walk through and over ANYTHING when we are with Him. Dear Christian, on your walk with God, you're going to have to keep your focus on Jesus. God has given us a hope in Christ, and that hope will lead you to your God designed destiny. It is imperative that you know today that the storms of your life will come, but you must keep your eyes focused on Christ so that you don't sink. Jesus says to us today do not be afraid because He is with you every step of the way.

> Focusing on Christ in your walk with God will keep you above troubled waters.

Reflections

Day 34

Get Your Gear On?

Romans 13:14

Have you ever seen a football player, at any level, play the sport without their gear on? Why not? In order to participate in the game, you need your gear on. In football, the gear list is as follows: helmet, shoulder pads, knee pads, and cleats. An athlete has to not only put their gear on, but also be disciplined when they compete not to beat themselves in the sport. Without the gear or the discipline, an athlete may be talented as ever, but they are not prepared to participate. Dear Christian, every day we must put on Christ and be prepared for what challenges life may bring to us. We must be disciplined to play the role God has for us. We have to put on the mind of Christ every day, because we need a Christ-like mindset in order to handle our challenges the same way Christ handled His challenges. We need the whole armor of God every single day because we are faced with trials all the time. Today's scripture says to put on Christ and make no provision for the flesh. That means that we can't try to put on God's gear and then play for another team. No matter how "together" we think we are, no matter how long we've been consistent in putting on Christ, we still must consciously put our gear on and go all out for Christ. Christ is coming any day, and we have to be prepared if we're going to play on His team.

We Need God's Gear to play on God's team.

Reflections

Day 35

A Christ-like Mindset

Phil 2:5

The mind is one of the most fascinating components of God's finest creation in mankind. The mind is not solely determined by your ethnicity or your upbringing but a conglomerate of factors. Although everyone has about the same size brain with the same number of neurons, people still tend to have different type of minds. Do you know what kind of mind you have? The main ingredient to the mind is the will. Jesus had a will to serve His Father. Jesus was *willing* to die so you could live. When Paul urges us to have the same mind that Christ had, He's telling us to have the same mindset. To be willing to go after God at all cost. To pursue God's will for our lives more than we pursue anything else. We can pursue credentials, careers, and commodities, but if we don't have the mindset of Christ, we will miss out on God's best for us in life. That mindset is one of humility and faith. There is nothing that can stop the person who has a mind set to accomplish the God-determined destiny for themselves.

> Nothing can stop you when your will is the same as God's will for your life.

Reflections

Day 36

What God has for you is Yours

Acts 10:34-40

Dear Christian,

Sometimes on our walk with God we tend to lose focus. We tend to look at other people and either see what they have, or what we don't have and lose sight of what God has for us. The scripture says today that God is no respecter of persons. That means that God does not show favoritism to anyone. God loves all of His kids the same. He has given all of us access to His promises. The great thing about God being our Father is that He never runs out of grace to provide for us all. We all can be full of His fullness, and God will still have plenty more for all of us. He has a perfect plan and destiny for us all. Jesus came for ALL OF US. Whenever you look around at others and see things that they have that you may like or want, remember it's not about the things. Seek ye first the kingdom of God and its righteousness, and all the other things shall be added (Matt 6:33). If God can bring someone else to something, He can assuredly do the same, if not more with you.

What God has for you is yours!

Reflections

Day 37

Finish Strong

1ˢᵗ Timothy 6:12, Jude 3

Vince Lombardi once said, "There can be no great victories in life, without great adversity." Dear Christian, every believer must earnestly contend for what they believe in at some point in their journey with the Lord. There will be many obstacles that will attempt to come against you, but you must be steadfast and unmovable. Putting your confidence in God means that when struggles come, regardless of what they look like, you have a strong belief and a boldness that your God will come through for you and be with you through the situation. In your walk with the Lord there are going to be times where we have to contend for our faith, but you CANNOT give up. Be faithful to the finish, continually look to God for help and strength, and keep your eternal prize and reward in your line of sight.

Stay the course by staying in faith!

Reflections

Day 38

Work It Out!

Exercise is good *for* your body! Exercise reduces risk from chronic illnesses such as diabetes, high blood pressure, and heart disease. Many of us know that exercise is good *for* us, but the reason why many people break their routine is because exercise is not necessarily good *to* us. Exercise can indeed be painful. As the old saying goes: no pain, no gain. There is no shortcut when it comes to transforming your physical body. Becoming stronger, faster, healthier, and more fit is a process and cannot be shortchanged to produce any long-term gain. Spiritual growth is a process much similar to exercise. Just like muscular strength is developed through consistent exercise, a person cannot grow spiritually without applying God's Word to their lives consistently.

We Have to Exercise Our Faith if we are going to walk with God.

Reflections

Day 39

You Are Special to God

Deut. 7:6

You are special to God. God has placed you on His priority list. God made you to bring Him glory. He wanted you to be born because He gave you a gift that the world needs. The special gift that God gave you wasn't given to anyone else because that gift He gave you is for a specific assignment that no one else can do or has ever done before. Have you ever wondered why everyone has different fingerprints? It's because what God has assigned to your hands no one else can touch or has ever been able to touch. God has chosen you to be special to Him. Because God has made you special to Himself, you can't live the way other people who don't live for God live. You cannot get caught up doing what other people who don't live for God do. When you become a part of God's family, you are In God's V.I.P. section of life. You are very important to God. The way you live your life should be a picture of what God is like when He fellowships with His special people.

Live like You Know you're special to God

Reflections

Day 40

Go!

Acts 26:16

God wants us to glow, grow, and go. He wants us to **Glow** in this dark world, **Grow** from spiritual infancy towards spiritual maturity, and **Go** witness to others the Gospel of Jesus Christ. God's kingdom purpose for all of us is to witness His-Story in our lives. The Gospel is the heart of God. He gave His only Son Jesus Christ for us to all fellowship with Him as His children. God has chosen you for such a time as this to serve others that precious Bread of Life, even the words of our Lord and Savior Jesus Christ, "I've come that they may have life, and have it more abundantly." (John 10:10) Rise up, dear Christian, and be a living epistle to your family, coworkers, and community. Share with others what God has shared with you. Don't be afraid or ashamed, God is with you, and He is leading you to the place He has prepared.

Walk by Faith, and experience God Today!

Reflections

Day 41

Transformed by Trials

James 1:2-4

All of us have been through a trial at some point in our lives. If you have not, don't worry, keep living. There is a common misconception that says that once a person, becomes a Christian, we no longer have to go through trials and tribulations. The Bible teaches quite the contrary. The Bible does not promise we will be free from trials or tribulations while on this earth. Rather, the Bible teaches that during adversity we will have favor, peace, and strength in our trials and tribulation. The Bible actually gives an example for us in the life of Christ. The trying of His faith transformed the world. Christ in His suffering for us on the Cross produced the perfect and entire work of Grace for all those who would put their faith in Him. In the same way, we all have to count it all joy because God can use our troubles to produce a perfect work within us. A coal has to be put under pressure makes a diamond, Gold has to be put under fire to be purified, and we as believer have to be tested to develop Christ-like character.

> God never promised we wouldn't go through fire.
> He promised that He would be with us in the Fire!

Reflections

Day 42

The Way Up is down

Luke 14:11

Humility is very important to God. God hates pride and loves humility. When a person is proud or boisterous, God is like, "Who are you to think that you are better than anyone else?" God created that person in His likeness just as much as He did you. When you try to exalt yourself, it's as if you're telling God that other people are not as important as you, and God doesn't like that. The Bible says, that God resists the proud, but He gives grace to the humble (1st Peter 5:5). Grace is like a super power from Heaven we need on our walk with the Lord. When we're proud, we shut off the power. The more we walk in humility, the more that power is given to us to manifest the will of God for our lives. The more we walk in that mindset of humility, the more we reflect Christ in our lives, which allows us to mature into the people God created us to be.

Pride leads away from God, Humility draws closer to God.

Reflections

Day 43

Growing Up

1st Corinthians 13:11

Most of us can remember when we were kids and can honestly say that time flew by so fast. Hopefully, we see the progression within ourselves and what all has changed about ourselves over the years. Things we did in elementary school we didn't do in middle school. Things we did in middle school we didn't do in high school, and if we went to college, there was a difference there from high school. The same is true in our spiritual journey. When we first come into Christ, our focus is mostly centered on ourselves and what Christ has done for us. As we mature in faith and love, we realize that Christ changed us so that we could be more of an example to others about what Christ is like. In that process of spending more time with God, we become more longsuffering, kind, humble, and honest. Our focus changes because it's not about us anymore. We become more passionate about others and more importantly, more passionate about others knowing Jesus. We can only stay at one place in our lives for so long. We can only stay in one place in our spiritual walk for so long before something has to change. Growing up is something we should look forward to and hope for because it's an eternity with God that's behind it.

God wants you to Grow Up in Him

Reflections

Day 44

Safety in Christ

Proverbs 18:10

Dear Christian,

I am sure there have been times in your life where you have felt as if you were surrounded by trouble. Nothing was going the way that it should. You were nervous, possibly tense, and very anxious. Naturally, you ran to your comfort zone to feel some sense of peace in the midst of your problem. Although what you ran to was not able to provide a solution, you still went to it for the sake of comfort. It briefly relieves you from the worry and fear of the reality of the situation. Regardless of if your comfort zone is ice cream, cookies, cakes, cheeseburgers, fried chicken, sports, alcohol, drugs, sex, etc. It can only temporarily please your emotions, but not permanently satisfy your soul. Our scripture today illustrates God as our ultimate strong tower. He is our refuge meaning in Him we are totally safe. When we go to God for help, he not only helps us with our issues, but He also grants us the peace that we need to settle our hearts and focus on the direction He has for us to go. We don't have to rely on temporary pleasures when we can have ultimate satisfaction and security in Christ.

> We have to leave our comfort zone to be comfortable with God.

Reflections

Day 45

Faith to Frame my World

Hebrews 11:1-3

When I was in high school, I used to go to school and sell snacks, sometimes even breakfast biscuits and drinks. I'll never forget my first time going to the store to purchase these items. I went to the store with my newly acquired bank card that I had just gotten a few hours earlier. Upon my arrival, I filled my buggy with goodies and got in line to pay. When I went to pay at the register, I swiped my new bank card. The card read declined! I asked the cashier to swipe again, and the card was declined again! I had no idea why it was reading declined. I felt so embarrassed and frustrated. I told the cashier my situation, and she asked me, "Did you activate your card after you received it?" I said, "No ma'am." She said, "Go get that fixed before I sell all these goodies to someone else!" Most people in society are filled with hopes, dreams, and visions, however when it comes time to cash in on their desires, the desires don't manifest because their faith is not activated. It takes faith to manifest desires. You can study, plan, have everything in place, but if there is no faith, the things you hope for will not come to fruition. It takes faith to please God and all of God's Promises are received by **faith** (Gal 3:14). Faith is the essential ingredient for life. Faith is the seen evidence of the unseen strategies. When you apply faith to your life, your world can be framed by your belief.

        Faith has to be activated before it's applied

Reflections

Day 46

Need it daily

James 1:5

I will never forget being in grade school. I used to be one of the kids who would try to go ahead and knock out my homework while I was still at school so I could play the rest of the evening. I remember one instance where the homework problems were really hard to me. I barely understood the concepts in class that day. While we had down time, I asked my teacher how to do the homework problems so I could get the work done correctly. When I did that, the teacher gave me exactly what I needed to successfully complete the assignment. Dear Christian, God is like that teacher. He will give you wisdom if you ask Him. God wants you to know that He wants you to know that you can come to Him with problems, and He will help you. He wants you to know what He is like so you can share Him other people. We don't have all the answers to every problem that comes up. We all need wisdom for every single day. We should ask God for His wisdom daily because He is going to help us and give us what we need to live life skillfully.

Ask God every day for His Wisdom!

Reflections

Day 47

An Eagle Eye Hope

2nd Thessalonians 2:16-17

One of an eagle's unique features is its ability to see from far distances. Its view in flight can spot a small rabbit over two miles away. Needless to say, an eagle is very far-sighted. In contrast, a lot of times we go through life, and have short-sighted hope. We wake up, go to class, and **hope** to get out of school early. Then, we get jobs and **hope** that we can get raises. We **hope** our favorite football team wins a championship, we **hope** our children turn out better than us, and we even **hope** we don't have to pay for them to go to college. On a day-to-day basis, we are **hoping** we get off work early, we **hope** our week goes by fast to get to the weekend, then we **hope** the pastor gets finished with his sermon before kickoff, etc. All of these hopes are short sighted, and not focused on the long term. We can be very short-sighted at times and miss out on God's best for us because we're focused on our present circumstances and not our hope in Christ. We tend to major in the minor things and minor in the major things when it comes to our focus. The scripture says that God will grant us everlasting consolation and a good hope through His grace. When you focus on Christ, He leads you through your problem to your promise.

Pray that God gives you an eagle eye of hope on your walk with Him Daily

Reflections

Day 48

Relationships pt. 1- Watch out

1st Corinthians 15:33

Watch your surroundings! Every person smiling in your face is not your friend, and every person that criticizes you is not your enemy. In every relationship, you are supposed to influence others towards a Godly life, not the other way around. Dear Christian, people will talk about you, say mean things to you, and even falsely accuse you, but you cannot allow your surroundings to influence you to go back into a lifestyle of sin. Some people do not provide an environment best for your spiritual growth, nor do they have your best interest at heart. People will come into your life and drain you. People will get close to you to get what you have, or keep you around them because they want to make sure you never accomplish more than them in life. Do not allow fear of rejection to cause you lose yourself. Be responsible, optimistic, and confident. God will bring the right relationships in your life, but you must be willing to walk away from the wrong relationships also.

When you're walking with God, sometimes you're going to have to walk away from some people, places, and things to get where He desires you to be.

Reflections

Day 49

Relationships pt. 2- Me and Others

Proverbs 13:20

As we discussed yesterday, relationships can either pull you towards God or away from Him. Our responsibility as believers should be to pull others towards God, not away from Him. Discernment is needed when selecting your "team" or the people you intend to get close to. The relationships you have can determine much of the decisions you make as well as influence your attitude. Relationships are critical because we become similar to the people we involve ourselves with the most. You don't want to be heavily influenced by negative people, because you yourself will become more negative. You are to be the Godly influence and the righteous conscious in all of your relationships. Even though eagles and chickens are both birds, chickens cannot fly, and eagles don't live on the ground. You, dear Christian are like the eagle, not the chicken. Though there is similarity between the two birds, they live different lifestyles and see from a much different vantage point. When you are influenced by the wrong relationships you are like an eagle coddled in a chicken coop. That's not where you're supposed to be. Relationships are very important, and you want to be surrounded by people who can edify and encourage you on your journey.

> Seek the Lord and pray He adds to your life healthy relationships that will aid you in your faith journey.

Reflections

Day 50

Relationships pt. 3-Me and the Church

John 13:33-34

The Bible says that we as believers are the body of Christ. The Greek word for body is "soma" which means "community." When you think of a body, look at your own. Your body is composed of various cells, tissues, organs, and organ systems that all function on one accord. If you drop a dumbbell on your pinky toe, what happens? Your hands rush to console the toe immediately, and the ENTIRE body is affected by the pain. In other words, what happened did not just happen to the pinky toe, but it happened to you! What we do affects each other, and we are designed to be in fellowship with other Christians. We are literally the community of Christ, meaning that we cannot function in isolation. We as believers are knit together by the spirit the same way that our bodies are joined together by ligaments and bones. We must love and affirm other Christians, even if they do not go to our same church or are in another denomination. Christ has unified us into His body, and we have to function on one accord.

We are His Hands and His feet to carry His Work.

Reflections

Day 51

Relationships pt. 4- Me and Marriage

Ephesians 5: 22-28

So you knew this was coming right? Great, I'm glad you're prepared. All week long we have discussed different types of relationships and how to apply our faith in these situations. Today, we're talking about marriage, which can be touchy for many, but when we approach marriage we want to make one thing clear. Marriage is not about us, it's about God. Marriage is so powerful because it is designed to reflect the relationship between Christ and His Church. We as men and women cannot love each other truly if we don't love God. The only way we will truly show love towards our spouse is if we have received God's love for ourselves. In every relationship, especially marriage, the other person is supposed to get the overflow of your relationship with God. They can't get the overflow if you are empty. Moreover, two can't walk together except they agree (Amos 3). If you and your spouse are not both going into the **"God first"** direction for your lives individually, there will be many problems looming ahead. God desires for you to be happy, healthy, and holy. His love and His wisdom will guide you in the right direction, but you must be willing and obedient to make the turn for yourself so you can have the God-designed marriage.

Marriage is honorable and beautiful. When God is in it, He makes it GLORIOUS!

Reflections

Day 52

Relationships 101-pt. 5 Me and God

Matt 22:37-40

Dear Christian,

Jesus loves you more than you could ever imagine. He loves you so much He gave His life for you. He died the death that we ourselves deserve and lived the life that we could not live so that we wouldn't have to go through life on this earth without having a chance to experience true love, peace, or joy. Jesus is the source of all life, fulfillment, and satisfaction. The Bible says, in Him we live, move, and have our being (Acts 17:28), meaning that without Jesus there is literally no us. We can't know another person until we really and truly know ourselves. It's impossible to truly know ourselves if we really don't know Jesus. When we intentionally seek Christ and get to know Him through His Word and prayer, we discover what it means to be free from insecurity, fear, and hopelessness. This prepares us to develop healthy relationships with others, demonstrate the love of God and treat others the way we desire to be treated.

We can't love anyone else until we get to know God and love Him first.

Reflections

Day 53

A Solider in God's Army

2nd Timothy 2:3-4

A soldier is a highly trained warrior who fights as a part of an army on behalf of their nation. A soldier has to go through rigorous training and preparation for battle. A solider is trained how to combat, navigate, and communicate with their fellows in any circumstance. A soldier's focus is not typical civilian affairs such as shopping, having cookouts, watching certain tv shows or sports competitions. A soldier is not overly consumed with these types of affairs because they are focused on their mission their commanding officer has given them. Similarly we as believers in Christ should be focused on our mission, not overly consumed with the cares of this life. We should allow God to train us in His Word and pursue His mission for our lives, that is, what He has commissioned us to do as disciples and ambassadors for Jesus Christ. We are representatives of God, and our citizenship is of Heaven (Phil 3:20). God trains us to combat spiritual warfare, navigate through life skillfully, and communicate with other believers effectively. When we decide to represent God, we decide to become a part of God's invincible army.

    A good soldier in God's army prepares in prayer.

Reflections

Day 54

Onward Christian Soldiers

Ephesians 6:11-18

Dear Christian,

On your journey with God there will be times you will feel like you are stuck in a dry spot. There will be times where you will feel challenged in situations that will seem very uncomfortable. Sometimes we feel attacked and overwhelmed with problems that come against us. These are the times we must be prepared not only to defend ourselves from the enemy's attacks, but also to offensively go forward on our faith journey with God. The enemy wants you to remain discouraged and lose faith because He knows that without faith, we cannot walk with God. All he wants is that we don't make progress on our journey. However, when we confess God's Word and use it like a sword, we grab that shield of faith, understanding who we are in Christ as mighty warriors because we have such a great salvation. We've been redeemed by God's truth, covered in His righteousness, and have our steps ordered in His peace. There is no uncomfortable situation that we cannot overcome for we are MORE than overcomers in Christ.

We must go onward in our walk with God.

Reflections

Day 55

Grace in Godliness

Titus 2:11-14

The Grace of God is what enables a believer to live a godly life. Grace not only introduces a person to salvation, but also enables a believer to obey God's will. Grace teaches a believer how to make God first decisions and live a God first lifestyle. Grace is like a fully loaded vehicle. Think of your dream car, fully loaded. It has all the bells and whistles, all four tires, full tank of gas, air conditioning, good mileage, etc. Everything you need to live the way God wants you to live, you already have in His grace. The only thing we as believers have to do is believe in God to experience His divine power. God's grace will teach you and enable you to live a lifestyle that reflects God's character. His grace is more than enough for you to overcome any weaknesses you may have. Moreover, His grace will become perfect strength in the areas of your weakness. Grace is all you need to be all God wants you to be. Regardless of where you come from or what you did in the past, God's grace is sufficient and ever present to help you along your Christian journey.

His Grace leads you to a life of Godliness.

Reflections

Day 56

Proverbs 4:5-7

Wisdom is the Principal thing

Wisdom is mentioned in the Bible over 200 times. It must be something important. Many people look for wisdom all over but, people overlook it right here in God's word. It's not something that can be found from mainstream media, reading, or even listening to old people. God's Wisdom comes from God. If you are seeking wisdom for anything right now, I highly encourage you to pray for it diligently as well as read God's Word regularly to obtain God's Wisdom for living life skillfully. We cannot pray for wisdom too much. Wisdom is a foundational principal that every believer will need throughout their lifetime. God's wisdom is so important for us. God's wisdom will help you make the right decisions throughout your life. Wisdom will lead you to make decisions that will advance you much further in life opposed to if you didn't have it. God's Wisdom will be critical to help you make decisions that can determine the direction of your life. This is why we should pray for it daily and apply it to our lives with everything we do.

Wisdom is the ability to live life skillfully.

Reflections

Day 57

Jeremiah 17:7-8

Planted in My Purpose

When a seed is planted, it is planted with the expectation to become a tree and produce a harvest. Where the seed is planted is very important. The seed must be planted in a place most conducive for it to grow. Many of us have been planted in places that have not been conducive for our seed to grow. Many of us have planted seeds in places that were not conducive for the seeds growth. When a seed is planted in the wrong place, it can very easily die well before its time or produce a bad harvest. God says, the person who trusts Him will be like a tree that has been planted near water, which is the perfect location for a tree. The tree never misses a harvest season. It is lively and continually thriving, regardless of what season it is in. This is how God wants us to be every single day. When we plant our trust in God, He takes care of the harvest, and we produce much fruit for everyone connected to us to taste and see of the Lord's goodness.

Planting your trust in God will produce an eternal harvest you can't even imagine.

Reflections

Day 58

Marking The Trail

Proverbs 3:5-6

Now that you have made progress on your path, it's important to remain focused now more than ever. God wants you to demonstrate His compassion and character to others. Sometimes as we go along our path, we get sidetracked and distracted because our days are so full of *busy-ness*. We start putting off time with God, and we get in situations where we don't know what the right decision is. When an explorer goes hiking, they mark their trail along their journey so they have a reminder of where they went. Moreover, it helps others behind them not to get lost, but follow the path laid in front of them. We, as Christians at certain points in our spiritual journey should acknowledge the reality of where we were before we came to Christ, what has happened to us since we've come to Christ, and most importantly, where are we going as we follow Christ. Becoming born again is an experience, but walking with God throughout life is a journey. We can help others along the way by telling people what God has done in our lives and demonstrating Godly character. Continue to acknowledge God in every area of your life. Doing this will help you to narrow your focus and make the right decisions. Continue this process of seeking and following the Lord because, as you follow Him, others will follow you.

Follow God, and mark the trail for others to follow suit.

Reflections

Day 59

Matt 20:34

The Compassion of Christ

Compassion is something that we don't share much of today. It's like that bucket of popcorn you give your wife at the movies. Once you hand it to her, you never see it again. Compassion is demonstration of love. It's a heart for another person to grow and progress. Jesus had compassion on all kinds of people when He was on this earth. A sign of His compassion was His healing of the people. This is seen in His compassion for us. Every single day, Jesus is trying to show us His love and care through His Word and His people. Furthermore, in the same way Jesus had compassion on people, so should we have compassion on others so that God would be seen in us and others would be compelled to come to Jesus to receive Him as Lord and Savior. We should not look at people who are not born again as pet projects or enemies. We have to realize that we were in their same position at one time and show grace and compassion to them as was demonstrated to us. Being compassionate is not being passive or tolerable of sin. Being compassionate is intentionally sharing God's love and God's truth at the same time.

> A Christ-Centered Life is a life filled with Compassion.

Reflections

Day 60

Give God Some Time

John 12:24

Dear Christian,

Many times we get caught up in our busy lives and get confused. We mix up business with *busy-ness*. Somewhere along the road we get stuck in busyness thinking it is business and we get left with nothingness. Jesus gives us this illustration of understanding purpose and priority. He knew His purpose, and He prioritized his purpose above anything else. When the time came to accomplish His mission, He was able to do so. Our takeaway is that in the same way Jesus was able to prioritize His purpose and accomplish His mission, so must we have the same mindset to be willing to sacrifice something temporal in order to gain a far better prize. Jesus said, except a seed dies, or is sown in the ground, it cannot produce a harvest. You and I, except we deny ourselves for the sake of Christ, cannot reap God's promise. Neither can we grow spiritually if we don't practice spiritual disciplines. When we don't have any time for God, we don't have any presence of God. We must invest our time in God's presence if we want to experience His presence in our lives.

The Price of God's Presence is your time

Reflections

Day 61

Outward Trouble, Inward Transformation

2nd Corinthians 4:16

The Apostle Paul writes to the church at Corinth sharing the various trials he was going through. He was not complaining about them as most of us would do. Instead, he speaks of them with joy and zeal. He knows that the suffering he endures for Christ is nothing to be compared to what Christ did on his behalf. Moreover, what he suffered is nothing to be compared to the eternal reward in which he is striving to receive. Thankfully, we today don't have to go through as much as Paul did. However, when we do go through, we can be encouraged that enduring suffering for Christ's sake has a far greater reward than risk. Although outwardly we seem to be perishing, inwardly we are being renewed and strengthened. It's not about how we feel, it's about the perfecting of our faith.

> It's not about how we feel, it's about the perfecting of our faith.

Reflections

Day 62

The Gospel Message

Galatians 2:20

The Gospel is the power of God to salvation to everyone who believes (Romans 1:16). When we are without strength, the Gospel strengthens us and empowers us to live victoriously. The Bible says, all have sinned and fallen short of the Glory of God (Romans 3:23). Sin is breaking God's law, and the penalty of sin is death. Since all have sinned, everyone on earth faces death and eternal separation from God. God knows we're powerless on our own to overcome sin, so He sent His Son Jesus Christ to atone for our sins by dying in our place. His resurrection empowers us to overcome sin so we don't have to become victims of sin and death anymore. The life we live now that we are "saved" or "born again" is not our life, but it's the life of Christ who lives within us, showing us how to live in the righteousness of God. I don't have to earn God's acceptance or His righteousness. He has accepted me in Christ, and He has made me righteous because I am in Christ Jesus! The Good News to the sinner is that God accepts you just the way you are so He can clean you up, make you whole, and show the world your true beauty and purpose!

The Gospel takes us to our divine purpose and destiny!

Reflections

Day 63
Full Tank of Faith

Colossians 3:16

Cars need gas to function, and if you want to drive your car on a road trip, you need to make sure your car has a full tank of gas for travel. We as Christians, are on a journey through life, and all we need is faith in Christ to go from where we are to where God wants us to be. Many of us do not seem to be getting anywhere because we are trying to go through life without faith. It's like we're trying to travel on the highway with an empty gas tank. When our car is empty or low on gas, we typically find a nearby filling station so we can fill up our car with fuel so we can get back on the road. Unfortunately, many Christians are pulling into filling stations called churches around the world and aren't filling up, so when they attempt to get back on their spiritual journey they still feel weak making little to no progress. The Bible says "the just shall live by **faith**" (Romans 1:17). This is why we need God's Word every day, because it strengthens our faith. When we allow God's Word to dwell in our hearts richly, we become rich in faith. No matter what you're going through, stay full on faith. Don't get to a filling station and not get what you need. Remain in God's Word daily, and you will have more than enough to receive your promise.

We need a full tank of faith on our journey with God

Reflections

Day 64

Covenant vs. Contract

Hebrews 10:16-22

Contract- if one agreeing party violates the contract, the whole contract becomes null and void. Essentially, the signers of a contract agree to hold up their end as long as the other signatories hold up theirs also.

Covenant- both parties agree to hold up their end regardless of the other party. It doesn't matter as far as the other party's responsibility to continue to do what they agreed to do.

Many people think we have a contract with God. However, we forget that God has made a *covenant* with us. There's a difference. We assume that if we don't hold up our end, and fail, then, contractually, God won't hold up on His. As a result, we get discouraged in our spiritual journey because of our flaws. The standard of God is perfection, and we know we're not *practically* perfect. (Hebrews 8:10-13). But, the good news is we have a covenant relationship with God, not a contract. God has already committed to receiving us in light of Jesus' perfection when we choose to believe Him for who He is and what He's done for us. Understanding our covenant relationship with God is lived out by committing to Christ even when we make mistakes. It's saying even though I fell, God still loves me. Grace is **need based**. I **need** a savior. I can't save myself. Where my weaknesses are, I need His strength.

Relating to God in a covenantal framework is receiving love and grace as well as giving love and grace **unconditionally**.

Reflections

Day 65

Greatness from God's Perspective

Matthew 23:11

Service is not about ourselves, service is about helping others. Jesus wants us to live our lives with serving others in mind. God's intent with Jesus was not only to get through to you and me, dear Christian, but also to use you and I to get to others. God desires to use us every day to bring people of all races to Himself. God wants people to see Him through our lives. When we live lives of humility and compassion, God is honored and recognized because these are not natural attributes we display on a daily basis. People are naturally selfish, unnaturally selfless. We have to deny ourselves consistently. Jesus did not come to be served, rather to serve others. Dr. Martin Luther King Jr. once stated, "everyone can be great, because everyone can serve." Service is about putting others before yourself. Service for others promotes peace, harmony, and love above our ambitions. Every day, we have to humble ourselves to let Jesus be exalted in our lives. The best part about exalting Him is that He will lift us up also.

    Everyone can be great, because Everyone can serve!

Reflections

Day 66

Lord Have Mercy

Luke 6:36

Mercy is an extraordinary concept. It's what we don't deserve when we've done wrong. Jesus taught us to be merciful like our Heavenly Father is merciful (Matt 5:7). God did not have to send Jesus to die for us. We were living in sin and were people who disobeyed Him constantly. We broke God's laws every day! We all deserve to be punished, but God saw the problem of sin. We couldn't fulfill His laws. He had mercy on us by sending us Jesus. Now, we receive mercy when we fall. That's something to be thankful for! God has given us an opportunity to live and experience Him in all of His holiness when we clearly have fallen short of it. In the same regard we should extend mercy to people when they fall short of our expectations or make mistakes. Jesus said treat others the way you would want them to treat you, not treat people the way that they treat you. Dear Christian, how would you feel if God had no mercy on you?

Thank God for His Mercy.

Reflections

Day 67

I AM HEALED!

1st Peter 2:24

Dear Christian, Christ has come to heal all of your brokenness and pains. We all had a serious wound of sin. Jesus provided the perfect medicine of salvation to heal us from all of its effects and symptoms. You see, all of us have experienced being either wounded or seriously injured. When a wound is open, it hurts. A wound cannot just be covered. It must be treated with proper medication to undergo healing. If a wound is poked at prematurely, a wound can reopen and get infected. If infected, the wound can lead to death. When a wound is properly treated, the medication creates a cleansing and a restoring on the broken tissue, which leaves a scar. The scar itself does not mean that the wound is still untreated and deadly. The scar actually means that the wound is healed and is no longer an issue. The Gospel message is that God has healed us, and though we may have a scar from our sin, we can rest assure that our sin is no longer an issue. Moreover, we don't need to hide our scars because when others see our scars, we show them that healing is available for them also.

Let Jesus heal you

Reflections

Day 68

Matt 18:4

Child-like, not Childish

Humility is something that we all have to embrace. It starts with an acknowledgment that none of us are inherently humble. Inherently, we brag, we boast, we claim all the success but none of the failures. Since we were kids, we've been programmed to try and be cool. We got older, and the story is still the same. We want to fit in, have things that other people have, wear clothes that other people wear, have cars like our peers do, have families by a certain age like our peers, we compare ourselves to other people and feel like we have to compete with them for NO trophy. **That's childish**! When things don't go our way, we throw temper tantrums and act out. We tend to shift the blame towards others and be rebellious when we have problems. **That's Childish**! God, our heavenly Father, understands how tough it can be down here. He knows the struggle, that's why He has to teach us how to live. Just like a child has to be taught how to behave naturally, we have to be taught how to live this life spiritually. Humility means not being self-centered but rather purpose centered in how we prioritize our lives. Just like a child is full of faith, we need to be full of faith. God wants us to be like a child in faith but mature in character to become the people He created us to be.

God wants us to be child-like, not childish.

Reflections

Day 69

We Need Compassion

1 John 3:17

Compassion is not just a feeling sympathy or sorry for another person in trouble or who is less fortunate. Compassion is more so a strong desire to help people in need. Jesus personified compassion in his earthly ministry, as he went out, healed people, and delivered them from their various forms of bondage and depravity. Moreover, the Bible says in John 3:16, "For God so loved the world, He gave His only begotten son" … This act of giving out of love is a demonstration of God's compassion toward humanity. In our suffering, God had compassion on all of us and gave us Jesus to deliver us from our bondage and iniquity. The apostle Paul calls us to have compassion toward one another, being mindful of others, thinking of them more than ourselves. Galatians 6:2 says we should bear one another's burdens and fulfill the law of Christ. Before you embark on today's journey, dear Christian, make an intentional decision to make a difference for someone else and demonstrate the love of God in your character.

Compassion demonstrates the Character of God.

Reflections

Day 70
It's Not About the Stuff

Luke 12:15

Ok, so if you're anything like me, you like nice things. You may like to nice shoes, clothes, cars, jewelry, etc. There's nothing wrong with having these things. Lord knows I like my fair share. However, when we constantly seek these things, we lose focus on our priorities and what matters most in life. Jesus gives a warning because He knows that it's very easy for us to stray off the path He has for us when we get caught up with material possessions. In this life, we pursue what we see. In addition to this, we pursue possessions because we compare ourselves to others and try to either get the stuff they have or get better stuff than them. We are constantly trying to race or out-do people to no avail because there is no competition between you and them! The only competition we have is with ourselves. Be the best you, you can be every day. Don't try to compete with people who have no control over your life! You have your own grace to run your own race! Stop pursuing things and trying to add Christ. Start pursuing Christ and things will be added. There is so much more to life than possessions. There are so many dynamic relationships, networks, gifts, talents and experiences God has for you. Being caught up in material things will cause you to miss it all.

> Don't seek things and expect Christ to be added. Seek Christ and expect things to be added.

Reflections

Day 71

Share Your Gifts

1st Peter 4:10

Have you ever heard of the phrase "sharing is caring"? This is a true statement. When we share something with someone else, we indeed are extending something of ourselves for another person's benefit. God has made us all unique. Although we all have one call to represent Christ, we are not all the same. God is able to use all of us to reflect His glory in various ways. Just because you are not a pastor or church leader, never think you are not able to be used by God to witness, disciple, or minister to anyone at any time. You should share your God-given gift in a way that brings God glory. You can share your gift in a unique way and still manifest Christ in your life. We can't just stay in our Christian bubble to grow spiritually. There will be times where we are nudged by God to get out of our comfort zone. This nudging is a stretch of our faith. It ultimately works for our good so we can become more like Christ and so more people can see Jesus in how we live our lives. Don't be selfish with all the amazingness God has given you. Share it with someone else today, and experience God move in your life on another level.

Share God's love with others.

Reflections

Day 72

Commitment to Christ

Daniel 6:11

Daniel was not afraid to continue praying. Daniel did not bow to the king. Daniel was committed to his God more than his job. Daniel centered his day around his time with God, and he did not try to fit God into his day. When Daniel's circumstances changed, he did not change on God. We can take a lesson from Daniel and learn the importance of commitment to God above all else. When we prioritize God in our lives, there is no fire nor lion's den that we can be thrown in where God will not deliver us. The Bible says, when a man's ways please the Lord, He makes his enemies be at peace with him (Proverbs 16:7). Meaning, when we live lives pleasing to God, there's nothing that the enemy can throw at us to take our peace or hold against us.

Remain Committed to Christ. He WILL Deliver you from your trials.

Reflections

Day 73

The Word of Life

John 8:51

A battery that has life brings life to whatever it's connected to. In the same way, God's word is the battery we need for life. When we hear God's Word and receive it, we become empowered by God so that He can use us to function according to our purpose. Let's use a TV remote for example. When the battery is placed within the remote, the remote is used to control the TV. When the battery is removed from the remote, the remote is useless. In the same way, God has given us His word to be hid in our hearts so we won't sin against him (Psalms 119:11). When we don't have His word, we are lifeless and unable to be used by God for His work here on earth. We have to be fully charged on God's Word to live the way God intended for us and to fulfill the purpose God has created for us to accomplish.

God's Word is your battery for living.

Reflections

Day 74

Preparation for Manifestation

1st Timothy 2:15

The Apostle Paul in his last letter writes to Timothy, "*study, and show yourself approved to God*". Paul knew that he would no longer be with Timothy or be able to minister in Timothy's place. Paul reminds him of the importance of being prepared for his upcoming assignment because he has a responsibility to minister to others before God. We all have to be prepared for tests in school, tests at work, tests in church. Virtually, everything in life undergoes some form of testing. Toilet paper doesn't even come off the assembly line until it's been tested for perfection. Much similarly, for you young Christians, to be all that God wants you to be, you must undergo testing and be prepared when the opportunity comes for you to walk into your divine destiny! God has a plan for your life. He wants to order your steps and guide you by His Holy Spirit. For Him to lead you, you must be willing to submit and follow Him. The first step of preparation is seeking God's presence continually. Every day, you should pray to experience God's presence. Seeking His presence will bring you divine instruction. Commit to giving God your all, moment by moment, day by day. Give God your all every day. From there, God will prepare you for the manifestation of His Will.

Prayer and worship are positions of preparation for divine manifestation!

Reflections

Day 75

Real Friends to Walk With

Proverbs 27:5

Dear Christian,

Real friends are not people who smile in your face and tell you what you want to hear all the time. Likewise, real enemies are not people who say things to you that you do not like. For those who are married, you can grow a lot with your spouse if you would learn to listen and take their criticisms a little more seriously. We have to appreciate when we are being rebuked, criticized, corrected, and given instruction because true growth and development comes from out of our mistakes and poor decisions into a place of progression, correctness, accuracy, wisdom, and understanding. We see a glimpse of this truth in the life of Jesus when He rebuked Peter and called him Satan (Matt16:23). Jesus knew Peter was not Satan. He loved Peter, but He had to correct him and move forward with His mission. Real friends who love you will correct and rebuke you in order to keep you straight moving forward with your mission. Dear Christian, you need real friends in your life who will pray with and for you. You need real friends who will hold you accountable. You need real friends who will push you up and not bring you down. Dear Christian, real friends are gifts from God, and He will bless you with the right people in your life, but you must be able to appreciate them appropriately.

Real friends will walk with you on your walk with God.

Reflections

Day 76

Reliability of Scripture

Romans 1:20

Many Christians have questions about the Bible and its reliability. Today, we're going to examine a few evidences for you to share and grasp a tighter understanding of God's Word. Today's scripture discusses how the world clearly demonstrates God's glory in front of people. However, we know many people today are resistant towards God and claim they cannot trust what the Bible says. Today, I want to share with you a few notes to help you on your Christian journey. The first is the lesson of **Manuscripts**. The Bible is the most recorded and sited document in the world BY FAR. Over 26,000 manuscripts in comparison to 9, and 10 respectively for other notable writings like Shakespeare and Caesar. The next lesson is in the area of **Archaeology**. The Bible is the most archaeologically-proven document in history. Many places mentioned in the Bible still exist today, and many items mentioned in the Bible are now collected as artifacts. The third lesson is **Prophecies**. There are 1,817 mentioned in the Bible. Many of these prophecies have been fulfilled and proven true with Christ's earthly ministry. The final area we will examine today is the area of **Science.** The Law of Biogenesis states that life can only come from life. The Bible says that God [who is the source of all life] created the Heavens and the earth (Genesis 1:1).

God's Word is reliable and has the MAPS for your eternal destiny.

Reflections

Day 77

Be Courageous

Joshua 1:5

Young Christian, there are many battles ahead of you. There are many battles you will have to face, but you will not face these battles alone. God will be with you. All He asks you to do is be courageous and make the decisions that God wants you to make. Go into the endeavor in faith. God has not given you the spirit of fear, but one of power, love, and a sound mind (2nd timothy 1:7). You have great dreams. Your dreams were given you by God. To take possession of your dream, you must have courage. People will not like you, people will come against you. You have to remember Great Anointing is always Greatly Attacked. The enemy will try to attack you with his arsenal of doubt, unbelief, affliction, and temptations but No weapon formed against you shall prosper! (Isaiah 54:17) You will be victorious if you be courageous. God was with Abraham, Moses, Joshua, and David, and as surely as He was with them then, He is with you now.

You will be victorious. Just be courageous!

Reflections

Day 78

A Leap of Faith

Hebrews 11:6

I remember being a kid living with my grandmother. I would do all kinds of things, hide in all kinds of places, and eat all kinds of things (even some things that aren't supposed to be considered edible). I had so many innocent injuries because I was so inquisitive and curious about the world around me. I would seek after people to talk to me about their past, about school, about television movies, EVERYTHING! Well, God and His word is for certain. We don't have to question Him, but God does want us to seek Him and desire to learn more about Him through His Word and prayer. The Bible says that "*God is a rewarder of them who diligently seek Him*", and we need faith to do so. The faith is not faith in things, the faith is faith in God. God wants us to believe in Him and pursue Him first in our everyday lives. A leap of faith is a by-product of our relationship with God. As we follow His direction and leadership, we make choices and decisions that lead us closer into His presence. His rewards will follow.

Walking With God takes many leaps of faith.

Reflections

Day 79

Joy Unspeakable

Isaiah 12:3

There's a man in Angola prison right now sentenced to life in prison without the possibility of parole. When visited by a young Christian missionary, the man had a large smile on his face. The missionary asked him why he was smiling so much. The man told him how much he appreciated the opportunity to see the sun from the outside. He took joy in that his family had been writing him and that he had a visit from the missionary. He knew he was passing away, however, he said, "Everybody has to die. That's nothing new." He took the greatest joy in knowing he would transition from this world and be translated into eternity with His Heavenly Father. He said, "Despite all that has happened in my life, and all that I've done, God loves me, and talks to me every day". That's true freedom! Dear Christian, we have nothing to complain about and nothing to be afraid of. We have the greatest hope in Christ. We can take great joy in God's love for us. The world didn't give you this joy, and it can't take it away from you. We truly have an unspeakable joy in Christ! Even though we may seem bound by our failures, insecurities, and inabilities, we have our joy and strength in Jesus, which is worth more than the temporal conditions of this world.

There is great joy to be revealed in your walk with God.

Reflections

Day 80

The Path to Your Destiny

Jeremiah 6:16

Young Christian,

Your greatest concern may be to discover what you were made to do. The answer to your question is provided in God's Word. As you embark on your spiritual journey, you will begin to discover and experience revelation about God and about yourself. Pursue His Will for your life. He will lead you down a path of righteousness and will keep you in perfect peace. His plans for you are for peace and hope. Don't worry or get discouraged along the way because you have the author and perfecter of your faith with you every step of the way. Pursue Him through prayer, studying His Word, confessing His Word, worshiping Him, and Praising Him. Pursue God through your lifestyle, and He Will lead you to your destiny! Enter into His path for your life and live your life for God, not for money, fame, physical pleasure, or any other person. God has a path for YOU to take into your divine destiny. Walk with Him into it!

God is with you on His Path to your Promise.

Reflections

Day 81

God's Encounter

Exodus 3:4

Moses was by many accounts a failure of a person with His life. He was eighty years old when God showed up in the burning bush. He spent most of his life having not really accomplished anything. He had physical problems, and many people didn't have much good to say about Moses. Like Moses, many of us, when we have an encounter or a spiritual experience, are caught off guard because it's something we have never experienced before, and we immediately feel unworthy. Dear Christian, God does not use your past to determine where you're going in your future. He could have left Moses in the wilderness. But God saw beyond his mess-ups and saw His purpose for Moses. In the same way, God has set up this day for you to experience Him for the purpose that He has for your life. You may have not experienced a burning bush, but maybe a dream or a vision or a hearing of a still small voice has led you to this point where you are on the path God has for you. Dear Christian, everything is going to work out, simply hear and obey. Moses was afraid that He could not accomplish the task God gave him to deliver them and share with them what God said. There is no reason to fear, doubt, or fall away, I AM is with you and will help you fulfill HIS plan for your life. Experience God daily and He will lead you towards your destiny.

As I was with Moses, so shall I be with you. (Jos 1:5)

Reflections

Day 82
No Greater Love

John 15:13

In the OT, God's people did not have God's Spirit all the time. The Holy Spirit had not come yet because Jesus had not atoned for sin yet (John 16:7). God's presence was in the Holy Temple, and people could not enter the temple anytime they wanted. The temple was HOLY and only the High priest could enter into the temple once a year to provide sacrifices for the atonement of sins. When Jesus, our Faithful High Priest sacrificed Himself on the cross, He entered into the Holiest of Holies and made atonement for us. The Bible says, when Jesus was crucified, the veil, which represented the barrier between man and God's presence, was torn, that signified there would be no more separation between man and God's presence.

When a person receives Jesus into their heart for salvation, they immediately are considered God's temple because, as it was in the OT, When He dwelled in a temple. Now in the NT, He dwells on the inside of His people. Furthermore, Jesus called His disciples His friends because He had relationship and fellowship with them. God couldn't have it with His people in the OT, so it is with us, though Jesus is no longer with us in human form, we have Jesus in our hearts, and we can have fellowship with Him at any time! He wants you to know you can share with Him anytime about anything! He is with you, and He loves you so much.

What a friend we have in Jesus!

Reflections

Day 83

Break the Chain!

Matthew 18:21-22

Elephants are by far the largest and strongest animals on the planet. Elephants are caught and domesticated at an early age. They are chained in their infancy because their weaker and easier to control. As elephants grow older, they are much larger and stronger; however, by this time, they are ignorant of their strength. An elephant can easily crush a car or a small building with no problems, but they don't attempt to break free because they've been chained for so long they've don't know their strength and don't believe they can be set free. Many of us have been chained to our problems also, and we've been discouraged from seeking our deliverance. Dear Christian, Giving your heart and your hurt to Jesus will ensure your safety and freedom. Jesus said, "Come to me, you who are weary and heavy burdened, and I will give you rest" (Matthew 11:28) Whatever the hurt, whatever the issue, keeping that hurt in your heart is not going to help you. You can't take hold of your dreams if you are still holding on to your drama. Trust God to help you break every chain in your life.

The Chains are BROKEN.

Reflections

Day 84

Your MVP

John 14:26(AMP)

Every year in professional sports, coaches, general managers, and select people from the media decide whos the league's Most Valuable Player of the year. The most valuable player is the one who contributes the most to the teams success. As a Christian, Our MVP is the Holy Spirit. The Holy Spirit's ministry means so much to the believer, He is indeed the MVP of the Body of Christ. He brought us into the God's family, He comforts us when we feel afraid or insecure, He helps us, even with things we don't know we need help with, He intercedes on our behalf (We all have issues, even when we think we don't have issues), He's there to counsel us through moments where we need wisdom and guidance, He strengthens us when you're weak, He intercedes on our behalf, and He stands by us at all times! Without the Holy Spirit, we would be an Unholy Mess! The Holy Spirit is our MVP, and we need to keep Him active in our lives if we are going to accomplish anything that the Father has for us.

Keep the MVP in your life for successful Christian Living!

Reflections

Day 85

Everlasting Water

John 4:10-14

Water is essential to our lives in various aspects. Water keeps us clean, we need water to drink, and enormous amounts of water are used to power the electrical systems of some of our largest cities. We pretty much need water to live.

Have you ever been dehydrated? The first thing you're looking for isn't a soda can, you want some water! Your body is composed of 70% water! You have to drink at least 8 cups of water every day to be considered properly hydrated. Many of us are spiritually dehydrated. We are spiritually empty and deprived of our essential resource. Jesus told the woman at the well, the water He gives, no one would ever thirst after. I'd sure like to have some of that water! How about you? We can go to the well of God's presence through prayer Dear Christian, I encourage you to drink from the well of God's presence and be filled with the fullness of the Father. Let your soul overflow with peace, love, and joy in the Holy Spirit, and let God take you to the place of everlasting goodness.

Drink from Jesus' well of living water

Reflections

Day 86
JESUS IS MY ROLE MODEL!

John 14:12

For people who are much older than me, they can remember the playing days of Bill Russell, Kareem Abdul Jabar, Magic Johnson, and Larry Bird. All of these were great basketball players who became timeless sports figures. More than any of these, Michael Jordan rose above the rest and is still considered the best player in NBA history. In the Bible, we read about a lot of great people. People such as Moses, David, and the apostle Paul all were great men of faith who we still reference today throughout the scriptures. But far beyond all of these mentioned in the Bible, there is one person who exceeds all others. Jesus Christ stands out far more than any of the others because every other person has fallen short at some point. Jesus, however, lived a sinless, perfect life and died for all of our sins. No one else demonstrates a higher command of strength, love, self-control, and wisdom. Jesus is the true example for living, and this is why we should strive to be like Him.

The best part about us following Jesus is that it doesn't matter what mistakes we've made. Jesus sacrificed his life for all our sins and his blood makes us clean from all unrighteousness. Rest assured that your mistakes are not strong enough to separate you from God's love. You can follow Christ and re-present Jesus to the world at large!

Jesus is calling you to walk with Him on your Christian Journey.

Reflections

Day 87

Who Do You Want to Be Like?

Romans 5:19

Every person on the planet is either following Adam or Jesus. At one point, all of us had no choice but to follow Adam's path of sin. When Jesus Christ came to earth and atoned for our sins, we now have the option to follow Christ's path of salvation. Adam was disobedient to God's command not to touch the fruit of the tree. He blamed Eve for his sin because she gave him the fruit, which was actually blaming God for his sin because God gave Eve to him. Adam wouldn't accept responsibility for his actions. He was passive and allowed Eve to be tempted by the serpent when he could have stepped in to make sure they didn't disobey God. Jesus, on the other hand, accepted responsibility and was obedient to God bearing the cross. Jesus was NOT passive. He stood up for truth and righteousness whenever it was necessary. He lived very courageously. He knew he couldn't give into sin because He had your salvation at stake! Adam gave his life away for temporary satisfaction. Jesus, however, laid His life down for eternal reward. Again, I ask you, which of these do you want to pattern your life after? God has given you power over ALL temptations in Christ Jesus. Follow His path, and you will experience victorious living.

Who Are You Following?

Reflections

Day 88

Fruit of the Spirit

Gal 5:22-23

When I was a young boy, I used to work for my aunt on her farm every summer. On her farm, she had tomatoes, potatoes, soybeans, squash, watermelon, cabbage, all kinds of stuff. It's amazing what the ground will produce when you put a seed in it. Likewise, the Bible says that God's seed is in the believer (1st John 3:9) and just like my aunts farm with all that produce coming out of the ground, there are different characteristics that should spring out in the life of a born again Christian: Love, joy, peace, longsuffering, gentleness, goodness, faith, meekness, and temperance. All of these characteristics are the fruit of God's seed in a person's heart. They all manifest at different times and in different situations just like there are different seasons for different fruits and vegetables to be harvested. God's harvest never goes bad or gets stale. The fruit is always ready to be shared and received by anyone who would be willing to have it. God desires us to share His fruit with others. Have you ever heard people say, "I just need a little more peace" or something like that? You can be the one who gives them what they need! A word of encouragement and love may help someone come to Christ. As you embark on today's journey, please remember to bring plenty of spiritual fruit wherever you go so that all would taste of the Lord's goodness.

        Oh Taste and See that the Lord is GOOD!

Reflections

Day 89

His Grace is Sufficient

2nd Corinthians 12:9-10

Becoming born again is a life-changing experience. It leads a person to pursue their purpose on earth and eternity with Christ. It is only by God's grace we are able to become born again and enjoy the blessings of being God's child. Unfortunately, people forget about God's Grace and try to earn God's blessings. Your born-again life in Christ began by God's grace, and He is faithful to finish what He started in you BY His grace! God's grace is sufficient for you! Jesus said that His strength would be made perfect in your weaknesses. In other words, the harder the challenge for me, the more of God's strength I receive to stand against the problem! Dear Christian, on your walk with God, do not try to lean on your own understanding and ability. Lean on the sufficient superpower of God's grace to help you in your times of struggle. Rest in HIS grace, and trust that in Him you are: justified, set apart, and made stronger than any challenge you will face. His grace is ENOUGH!

Trust in God's Grace as we walk with Jesus into our Divine Destiny

Reflections

Day 90

Just Another Day?

Psalms 118:24

Most people complain about time. They complain that there isn't enough time in a day to get everything they need done. Yet, they STILL CHOOSE to push assignments and responsibilities off until later. If this describes you, I'm not bashing you, just making a point. Most people take time for granted, and they shouldn't. Everyone on the planet has the same amount of time. What you do with your time is your choice. Every day you wake up is a blessing from God. You can either waste that time or invest that time. Every day that you wake up, God has given you everything you need in the day to accomplish HIS PURPOSE for you in THAT day! Be careful not to get caught up in the thinking that there's nothing special about a new day. There is SO MUCH God has in store for you every day of your life. Don't allow anyone or anything to detour your focus from seeing God's goodness for your life EVERY SINGLE DAY. Stewart your time wisely, don't miss out on any opportunities to glorify God. Every day brings with it its own uniqueness and challenges. This is why we shouldn't think of the next day as "another day" because it's totally different than the previous days before it. Remember, it's a New day. It is totally new to everyone in the world. God has an assignment just for you TODAY. Find it and fulfill it!

God has purpose for you, TODAY!

Reflections

Day 91

Faith for Eternity-Destined for Glory

2nd Corinthians 5:8

At the beginning of the school year, I think the thought in every child's head at some point during the first day of school is, "I can't wait for summer!" Kids are longing to be done with school to enjoy the summer and not worry about homework. Unfortunately, the fun is only going to last a few months. Similarly, we, as Christians, should have a longing to be in Heaven for an eternity with God in ultimate Glory. This longing desire we should have is not going to only last for a short while, but for all eternity. That doesn't mean we just wait around here on earth and do nothing with our lives. Instead, we should live our lives with a sense of purpose and destiny. We should not just live to be successful, but also to impact our world for Jesus and leave a legacy for the next generation to follow. It starts with a vision that is carried out by faith and manifested by God's grace. This life has many challenges, but Jesus said, "Be of Good Cheer" (John 16:33). We have victory over every trial and challenge. What do you want your life to look like when you make it at the end? What dreams, goals, and assignments did God give you that you haven't accomplished yet? Seek to fulfill that dream and desire for God's glory now so that you will be prepared to
spend eternity with your Creator and experience your ULTIMATE DESTINATION in GLORY!

> Walking With God is a never-ending journey towards ULTIMATE GLORY!

Reflections

Prayer

Dear Lord, thank you for walking with me daily. Forgive me of my sins, and renew my heart. Order my decisions in your word. Lead me in your righteous path, and may you be pleased by my life.

Thank You Lord, for your grace and mercy. Thank You Lord, for your love. As I continue this journey, be with me. Give me a heart to serve and love like you every day of my life.

Fill me with your Spirit and restore my soul. Thank You Father, In Jesus name, Amen.

About The Author

Jameson Alston (24) is a native of both Oak Grove and Baton Rouge, Louisiana. Jameson is a young minister with interests in missions and service. He is a self-published author and songwriter. Jameson holds both his Bachelor's and Master's degrees from the University of Louisiana at Monroe (ULM), and is currently pursuing his doctorate in Physical Therapy. He loves reading, writing, and physical fitness. Jameson serves in ministry under the leadership of his pastor, Supt. Dr. Mark Ellis Sr. at United Christian Faith Ministries in Baton Rouge. Jameson desires to reach the world for Christ through writing, speaking, and missions both locally and globally. His mission statement is "to be the son God desires, an example to his brothers and sisters in Christ, and to be a light to the lost." Jameson is married to his lovely wife, Sharmaine Alston.

LET'S GET CONNECTED

Follow Jameson Alston on all social media platforms

Facebook: Jameson Alston
Instagram: @JAlstonSpeaks
Twitter: @JAlstonSpeaks
YouTube: Jameson Alston

www.ingramcontent.com/pod-product-compliance
Lightning Source LLC
Chambersburg PA
CBHW020531080526
44583CB00013B/819